# DIVINE MERCY

## IN THE SECOND GREATEST STORY EVER TOLD

### GUIDEBOOK

*Questions for Review and Discussion*

Fr. Michael Gaitley, MIC

*Jesus, I Trust in You*

*Nihil Obstat*: Fr. Luis Granados, DCJM, S.T.D. *Censor Deputatus*
*Imprimatur*: Most Reverend Samuel J. Aquila, S.T.L., Archbishop of Denver
December 9, 2015

*Imprimi Potest*:
Very Rev. Kazimierz Chwalek, MIC
Provincial Superior
The Blessed Virgin Mary, Mother of Mercy Province
November 16, 2015

Writers: Fr. Michael E. Gaitley, MIC, and Paul McCusker
Media Production: Steven Flanigan, Justin Leddick, Ted Mast, Kevin Mallory, Aurora Cerulli, Matthew Krekeler, Lucas Pollice, Connie Graves, and John Schmidt.
Print Production: Ann Diaz, Sarah Chichester, Brenda Kraft, Jane Myers, and Devin Schadt

**Augustine Institute**
6160 South Syracuse Way, Suite 310
Greenwood Village, CO 80111
Information: 303-937-4420

AugustineInstitute.org
Formed.org

**Marian Helpers Center**
Stockbridge, MA 01263
Prayerline: 1-800-804-3823
HAPP: 1-877-200-4277
www.TheDivineMercy.org
www.MarianMissionaries.org
**www.AllHeartsAfire.org**

Printed in the United States of America
978-0-9966768-7-8

# CONTENTS

*Jesus, I Trust in You*

# ACKNOWLEDGMENTS

Divine Mercy is not something new. Rather, it's the very heart of the Gospel. Still, the Holy Spirit has been working overtime in our day to draw our attention to a consoling and remarkable fact: *Now is the time of mercy*. In other words, now is a time of great and extraordinary grace for the Church and the world.

But it's not just the Holy Spirit who has been working overtime. There are several apostles of mercy who have generously poured themselves out to make this good news known.

In particular, I'd like to thank the video production team at the Augustine Institute, who put in long and grueling hours to make the videos better than I ever could have imagined: Steven Flanigan, Justin Leddick, Ted Mast, Kevin Mallory, Aurora Cerulli, Matthew Krekeler, Lucas Pollice, Connie Graves, and John Schmidt.

Also, I'd like to thank all those who contributed to this *Guidebook* through their comments, input, editorial work, artistic assistance, and prayers, especially Paul McCusker (who wrote the session introductions, conclusions, and prayers), Carol Younger (who offered particularly insightful suggestions for each session's questions), Sarah Chichester, Ann Diaz, Brenda Kraft, Jane Myers, Devin Schadt, and the Marian Missionaries of Divine Mercy, particularly Lewis and Michelle Brooks, Mark Cook, Eric Mahl, Brian Gail, Jr., Br. David Guza, OMV, Daniel Pendergrass, Joseph Gohring, Nicholas Sully, Martin Jankowski, Kimberly Harmon, Julie Musselman, and Amanda Ciccocioppo.

Finally, I'd like to thank Mark Middendorf for introducing me to Tim Gray, president of the Augustine Institute, who with my provincial superior, Fr. Kazimierz Chwalek, MIC, graciously made this collaboration possible for the glory of God's amazing mercy.

Fr. Michael E. Gaitley, MIC, STL
National Shrine of The Divine Mercy
Stockbridge, Massachusetts
December 8, 2015
Beginning of the Jubilee Year of Mercy

*Jesus, I Trust in You*

# INTRODUCTION

Welcome to the simplest and easiest small-group program we've ever put together! The purpose of this introduction is to tell you just how easy it is to use this *Guidebook* and participate in the program *Divine Mercy in the Second Greatest Story Ever Told*. But before we begin, I should first say something about how this program ties in with our other Hearts Afire Programs.

## A. Regarding Hearts Afire

If you've never done a Hearts Afire Program, don't worry. This *Divine Mercy* program *does* stand alone. However, it's also intended to be part of Hearts Afire: Parish-based Programs from the Marian Fathers of the Immaculate Conception (HAPP®), and that's really the best way to experience it. So, let me tell you about HAPP.

WHAT IS HAPP? As a whole, HAPP is presently the most popular complete, Catholic adult faith-formation program available in North America. Put differently, it's one of the most effective ways for laypeople to come together and grow in their faith in an ordered and deliberate manner that basically covers *everything*.

HAPP is structured on the four pillars of formation used to train priests in seminaries around the world. Those pillars are as follows: (1) spiritual, (2) intellectual, (3) pastoral, and (4) human.

The programs begin with *spiritual formation* through two small-group retreats based on the books *33 Days to Morning Glory* and *Consoling the Heart of Jesus*. These retreats focus on developing a deep, personal relationship with Jesus in his mercy, through Mary. Next, the *intellectual formation* begins with a small-group study based on the book *The 'One Thing' Is Three*, which covers the entire scope of Catholic theology. The focus then turns to *pastoral formation* through the reading and group discussion of the book *You Did It to Me*, which is a practical guide to putting mercy into action. Finally, *human formation* takes place through the small-group meetings themselves, which engage the participants in listening and sharing from the heart. (For more information about HAPP, see AllHeartsAfire.org.)

Best of all, just as a seminarian would graduate from his time of formation in the seminary and become something special (a priest), so also, anyone who completes the formation described above can also become something special (a Marian Missionary of Divine Mercy).

*Jesus, I Trust in You*

The Marian Missionaries of Divine Mercy is an organization that takes everything from HAPP formation and incorporates it into a spirituality, community, and way of life appropriate for laypeople. (For more information, visit MarianMissionaries.org and get the free *Missionary Handbook*.)

WHAT DOES THIS *DIVINE MERCY* PROGRAM HAVE TO DO WITH HAPP? While this *Divine Mercy in the Second Greatest Story Ever Told* (hereafter referred to as *Divine Mercy*) program is technically not one of the stages of formation of our Hearts Afire Parish-based Programs, it does serve those programs in three ways.

First, *Divine Mercy* provides *a powerful introduction to HAPP*, because it gives the historical background to everything that HAPP is about. More specifically, this program clearly reveals that *now is the time of mercy*. It tells the story of the great graces that God is giving to the Church and to the world in our time. For instance, it tells the story of the Divine Mercy message and devotion and Marian consecration, both of which comprise the backbone of HAPP.

Second, *Divine Mercy* provides *a powerful supplementary program to HAPP that can be inserted into any stage of HAPP*. For instance, let's say your group does HAPP programs in the fall and spring. Well, this *Divine Mercy* group program could be offered in the summer as an interim step to those other programs.

Third and finally, *Divine Mercy* provides *a cap or conclusion to HAPP and prepares people to become Marian Missionaries of Divine Mercy*. For example, after completing *The 'One Thing' Is Three* group study and *You Did It to Me*, your group could participate in *Divine Mercy* as a kind of preparation for becoming a Marian Missionary of Divine Mercy. (To become a Marian Missionary, one should already have read the book *The Second Greatest Story Ever Told: Now Is the Time of Mercy* or have participated in this group program.)

## B. About This Divine Mercy Program

THE VIDEOS. The 10-part video series *Divine Mercy in the Second Greatest Story Ever Told* is based on my book, *The Second Greatest Story Ever Told*. Now, whether you've read the book or not, you're in for quite a treat.

Our friends at the Augustine Institute have put together one of the most amazing visual presentations of one of the greatest stories ever told, such that you don't just watch it, you experience it. Really. They've brought to life the drama and splendor of God's merciful love revealed in Sacred Scripture, manifested at key moments of Church history, and realized in our present time of mercy. They've brought the book to life in a way that has left my staff and me filled with wonder and awe.

Part of what makes the Augustine Institute's video experience so engaging is that, true to the book, it's so fast-paced and covers a lot of ground. However, for that same reason, it can be a challenge to take so much material to heart. As one of the producers put it, "It's like trying to drink water from a firehose — but you want to drink all that water because it's so good!" And he was right. You'll really want to drink up, digest, and discuss the life lessons of *Divine Mercy*.

Well, that's where this small-group *Guidebook* comes in.

THE GUIDEBOOK QUESTIONS. This *Guidebook* essentially consists of eight questions for group discussion each week. However, there are several things about *the way* the questions are written that call for further explanation.

First, as you thumb through this *Guidebook*, you'll notice that the questions themselves are in boldface type and usually come at the end of a lengthy paragraph. (The exception is the first question, which is the same for each week.) The material leading up to each question not only provides an introduction to the question but also engages the mind by highlighting and reviewing key points from the videos.

Second, the questions themselves are not meant to be quizzes of your knowledge of the content. Rather, they're intended to help group members each make the content of the video their own through sharing. Put differently, the goal of the questions is to engage the heart. With both the mind and the *heart* engaged, there's no need for a quiz.

Third, it is not necessary to get through all the questions during the group discussion (and most groups probably won't). However, if your group does not get through all the questions, then everyone's homework will be to read through and reflect on the remaining ones. This is very important! Doing such homework will ensure that no one misses out on any of the key points. (I give a reminder to do this at the end of each week's group questions.)

THE PEOPLE INVOLVED. To effectively run a *Divine Mercy in the Second Greatest Story Ever Told* small-group program, you'll need three key people or groups of people.

1. The Program Coordinator. This person initiates and organizes the program (alone or with the help of others). Responsibilities would include picking the dates for the meetings, coordinating the participant materials (such as this *Guidebook* and the DVDs or access to the program on FORMED.org), finding a venue (with viewing screen), promoting the program, and selecting the Small-Group Leaders (if there are going to be several small groups).

2. Small-Group Leader. This person, selected by the Program Coordinator, leads the small-group discussion. (Of course, the Program Coordinator can also be the Small-Group Leader.) The primary responsibility of the Small-Group Leader is to read aloud the questions for the small-group discussion as the group reads along in their own *Guidebook*. The Small-Group Leader should also read the Appendix, "Information for Small-Group Leaders."

3. Participants. These are the people who come to the meetings to watch the videos and participate in the discussion. Each participant should have his or her own *Guidebook* so as to follow along as the questions are read and to later review any questions not covered during the discussion.

THE FIVE STEPS. Each week, when your group gathers to watch the video and have discussion, you'll follow five simple steps, which are as follows:

1. Opening Prayer. All the small-group participants join the Program Coordinator in making the Sign of the Cross, and then, together, everyone reads the Opening Prayer provided in this *Guidebook*.

2. Introduction. The Program Coordinator reads the brief Introduction aloud to everyone. (During the first meeting, the video portion is shorter than usual, which gives time to go over the "Ten Commandments for Small-Group Success" from the Appendix before watching the video.)

3. Video. The whole group attentively watches the video.

4. Small-Group Discussion. After the video, participants will break up into small groups of about 5-9 people. (If there are less than 10 people total, then there would only be one group.) The discussion will be based on the appropriate week's small-group questions provided in this *Guidebook* and should last about 45 minutes.

5. Conclusion and Closing Prayer. After the time allotted for the small-group discussion, the Program Coordinator calls everyone back to meet as one group, reads that week's Conclusion, and invites everyone to join in to pray the Closing Prayer.

[Please note: The participants in this program have no homework from week to week other than reading and pondering any questions that their group didn't cover during the group discussion.]

## C. The Book Version and More

This program only requires the videos and this *Guidebook*, but participants may also be interested in getting the book on which this video series is based. As I mentioned earlier, it's called *The Second Greatest Story Ever Told: Now Is the Time of Mercy*. To learn more about that book and other Divine Mercy resources, see the Resource Pages at the end of this *Guidebook*.

Now, I hope you and your group will enjoy watching and discussing *Divine Mercy in the Second Greatest Story Ever Told*. God bless you!

*Jesus, I Trust in You*

Jesus, I Trust in You

# SESSION ONE

## GOD'S SCHOOL OF TRUST

**Step 1**

## INTRODUCTION

To fully appreciate *Divine Mercy in the Second Greatest Story Ever Told*, we have to remind ourselves of the *first* greatest story. That amazing story sets the stage for the dramatic events that will unfold later in history.

**Step 2**

## OPENING PRAYER

*Heavenly Father,*
*as we begin this study of your merciful love for us,*
*please fill us with your grace.*
*Send your Holy Spirit to enlighten our minds*
*and enkindle our hearts*
*that we may be transformed by your mercy.*
*Help us to trust in your mercy, receive your mercy,*
*and be merciful to others.*
*We ask this in the name of our merciful Savior,*
*Jesus Christ, our Lord.*

*Mary, our Mother of Mercy, we entrust to you ourselves*
*and this time together. Please pray for us.*

**Step 3**

## VIEW VIDEO FOR EPISODE 1

*Before watching the video, together read through the*
*"Ten Commandments for Small-Group Success" in the Appendix.*
*Then, watch Episode 1. (This episode's video is shorter, so you'll*
*have extra time.)*

# SMALL-GROUP DISCUSSION

*[Go over these questions in your small group. It's alright if your group only gets through a few of them during your discussion.]*

1. **What was your favorite part from the video? In other words, what most touched your heart or enlightened your mind?**

2. This study centers around St. John Paul the Great as the Second Greatest Story Ever Told. More specifically, it's about the most important part of John Paul's life: Divine Mercy. *So, how has Divine Mercy affected you? For instance, as happened to Pope Francis at the time of his conversion after going to Confession, have you ever experienced the loving gaze of Jesus on you? Or have you been touched by the Divine Mercy message and devotion?*

3. God seems to be giving us the Second Greatest Story in our day for an important reason. Specifically, he wants to convince us that *now is the time of mercy*, that now is a time of great and extraordinary grace for the Church and the world. In fact, he seems to be telling us that he desires to give us unprecedented grace and mercy in response to the unprecedented evil in our modern world. *Alright, so if now really is the time of mercy, what specific gifts of mercy do you want from Jesus in your life? In the lives of others? In the life of a particular loved one?*

4. All of Salvation History can be summarized as a School of Trust, as God's great effort of trying to get us skittish, fearful creatures to give up our fear of him and to trust in his love and goodness. *Describe how God has shown his merciful love to you in your life and so earned your trust. Perhaps it was a situation where everything seemed hopeless, and then, suddenly, it all worked out in a way that only God could have done.*

5. It's not always easy to trust in God, and the reason goes back to Genesis and the wound from humanity's first sin. That original sin caused us to have a distorted image of God that makes us hide from him, like Adam and Eve. *So, can you think of one way that you have run away from God or hid from him in the past? Also, how can you avoid hiding from him in the future?*

## SMALL-GROUP DISCUSSION

6. A contract is an exchange of goods or services. A covenant is an exchange of *persons*. Now, the Bible teaches that God is constantly giving himself to us in covenant and that he wants us to give ourselves back to him. And even if we are unfaithful, he remains faithful. In other words, he doesn't stop giving himself to us even when we turn away from him. ***So, do you trust God enough to give yourself to him? What areas in your life have you not given over to him? Or what areas of your life do you struggle with giving over to him?***

7. At the time of Israel's greatest sin (the worship of the Golden Calf), God could have revealed divine wrath. But Moses interceded for his people and reminded God of his promise of faithfulness to Abraham, Isaac, and Israel. So, instead, God relented and revealed Divine Mercy, and revealed how he is always faithful to his promises. Specifically, he declared to Moses that he was a "God merciful and gracious, slow to anger, and abounding in steadfast love and faithfulness" (Exodus 34:6). This is a hugely important revelation! It tells us who God is as the darkness of our own sins swirls around us. ***To help ponder this glorious revelation, pick the one description of God in the passage from Exodus that most touches your heart. Is it "merciful," "gracious," "slow to anger," "abounding in steadfast love," or "abounding in faithfulness"? Why did you pick the one that you did, and what does it mean to you?***

8. Regarding that revelation of God's mercy in Exodus 34:6, St. John Paul II explained that Israel often found strength in that revelation during difficult times. Specifically, he said that the Israelites would actually *remind God* himself of that revelation of his mercy! Imagine that. Think of one of God's people saying to him, "Now, Lord, I've really blown it here, but please don't forget how you promised to be merciful to me!" And God heard those prayers. ***Have you ever prayed in such a way to God? In other words, in times of difficulty, have you ever reminded God about what he has revealed about his mercy? During such prayer, what specific things would you remind God regarding his mercy?***

> *Homework: Don't forget to read and reflect on all the questions that you don't cover during your small-group discussion!*

## CONCLUSION

In this first session, we learned that one of God's main activities since the fall of Adam and Eve in the Garden has been to convince us to place all our trust in him. Now, according to St. John Paul the Great, *mercy* is the central revelation, the central lesson in God's School of Trust. And that "school" is teaching us how, in the face of great infidelity and sin, God remains "merciful and gracious, slow to anger, and abounding in steadfast love and faithfulness." But school is still in session, and we have quite a way to go to better understand his incredible mercy.

## CLOSING PRAYER

*Thank you, Heavenly Father,*
*for your tireless efforts to pursue us with your mercy.*
*We thank you that, while we are yet sinners,*
*you take action to find us, to save us,*
*and to make us your own.*
*Give us clear minds and pure hearts*
*to see you as you really are: Love and Mercy itself.*
*Help us to be truly grateful for the many men and women*
*who have carried your message of mercy to the world.*
*We give you thanks for all your gifts,*
*Almighty God, who lives and reigns now and forever.*
*Amen.*

Karla — Gods School of Mercy.

## NOTES

_____

_____

_____

_____

_____

_____

_____

_____

_____

_____

_____

_____

_____

_____

_____

_____

_____

_____

_____

_____

_____

Jesus, I Trust in You

# SESSION TWO

## BEHOLD, THIS HEART

## Step 1 — INTRODUCTION

In Session One, we learned that the fall of man in the Garden of Eden has distorted our image of God and that the rest of the Bible can then be seen as God's tireless effort to try to heal that distorted image. We heard how that effort, God's School of Trust, appeared in the Old Testament through God's steadfast love and mercy toward the often rebellious people of Israel. Now, in this session, we turn our attention to God's School of Trust in the *New Testament* and to key moments of Church history.

## Step 2 — OPENING PRAYER

*Our Creator, the true fountain of light and wisdom,*
*pour upon the darkness of our understanding*
*the profound beam of your brightness.*
*Remove from us the darkness of sin and ignorance*
*into which we were born.*
*Give eloquence to our tongues and the grace*
*of your blessing upon our lips.*
*Give us quickness of understanding,*
*the capacity to retain what we learn,*
*the discernment to interpret what we hear,*
*and the facility to learn.*
*Guide us as we begin, as we go forward, and as we depart.*
*Through Christ our Lord. Amen.*

— Adapted from St. Thomas Aquinas's Prayer Before Study

## Step 3 — VIEW VIDEO FOR EPISODE 2

# SMALL-GROUP DISCUSSION

Step 4

*[Go over these questions in your small group. It's alright if your group only gets through a few of them during your discussion.]*

1. **What was your favorite part from the video? In other words, what most touched your heart or enlightened your mind?**

2. As we saw in the video, Jesus teaches us to trust in God through the lesson of his humble birth, through the way he reaches out to the weak, broken, and lost, through his suffering and Death on the Cross, through his glorious Resurrection, depicted in the image of Divine Mercy, and through his loving, ongoing presence in the Eucharist. *Which of these lessons most inspires you to trust in God? Why?*

3. Jansenism teaches that we have to earn God's love and be perfect before we can go to him, and promoted the idea that one must have absolutely perfect contrition before even approaching the Sacrament of Penance. It confirms and strengthens the false image of God that results from original sin — the false image of a God who is just out to ruin our fun and harshly discipline us for the slightest infraction of his many rules. *Has Jansenist thinking ever affected you? For instance, have you ever been fearful that God would stop loving you if you didn't say this or that prayer? How has Jansenist thinking affected your attitudes, your relationship with others, or your relationship with God?*

4. Jansenism breaks the Lord's heart and inspired the revelation of the Sacred Heart of Jesus to St. Margaret Mary Alacoque. Jesus said to her:

> Behold, this Heart, that so deeply loves mankind, that it spared no means of proof — wearing itself out until it was utterly spent! This meets with scant appreciation from most of them; all I get back is ingratitude — witness their irreverence, their sacrileges, their coldness and contempt for me in this Sacrament of Love. ...
>
> This hurts me more than everything I suffered in my passion. Even a little love from them in return — and I should regard all that I have done for them as next to nothing, and look for a way of doing still more. But no; all my eager efforts for their welfare meet with nothing but coldness and dislike. Do me the kindness, then — you, at least — of making up for all their ingratitude, as far as you can.
>
> —from the autobiography of St. Margaret Mary Alaccoque

*Does it surprise you that the Lord is brokenhearted over your lack of love? How do you feel about that? How might it change the way you pray?*

5. When he was a Catholic priest, Martin Luther suffered from a Jansenist-like spirituality, but then he found freedom through faith in the saving grace and mercy of Jesus Christ. That's great! But then he erred by leaving the Church, saying we are saved by faith *alone*, and by calling the Epistle of St. James an "epistle of straw." (He called it that because it contradicted his own teaching by saying that "faith without works is dead.") *Like Martin Luther, in your zeal for finding a spiritual insight or ideal, have you ever neglected something important? For instance, in your zeal for prayer, have you ever neglected your family? Or in your zeal to serve your family, have you ever neglected your duties toward God or toward those outside of your family?*

6. In response to Martin Luther, some Catholics emphasized the role of works so much that it seems they forgot the importance of faith. Today, this sometimes comes in the form of people who do lots of things that are surely good, but who don't have much of a personal relationship with Christ in prayer. Yet, such a personal relationship gets to the heart of Christian spirituality. *So, how would you characterize your personal relationship with Jesus? For instance, is he your best friend? If not, then why not? Do you speak to him daily from your heart? If so, then when?*

7. Saint Alphonsus de Liguori labored for many years (especially through his talent for writing) to make known the mercy of God within the field of moral theology. *What can you do to make known the mercy of God using your own talents? In other words, how might you help others to develop a personal relationship with Jesus and come to know his love for them?*

8. Saint Thérèse of Lisieux has been called "the Catholic response to the Protestant Reformation" because of how she helps Catholics to rediscover the primacy of faith in the spiritual life. Unlike Martin Luther, though, she does this without dismissing the saving importance of good works. *What do you know (besides what we learned in the video) about this remarkable Doctor of the Church? How has her teaching, such as the Little Way, affected your life?*

> Homework: Don't forget to read and reflect on all the questions that you don't cover during your small-group discussion!

## CONCLUSION

This chapter in God's School of Trust showed us the New Testament depiction of Jesus as loving and merciful, which helps correct our distorted image of God. Yet we also saw how the distorted image of God has come up again and again in Church history and how God countered that distortion by revealing the Sacred Heart. But that's not all. He also raised up great saints to combat Jansenism and remind God's people of his School of Trust, such as the ones we heard about in this episode. And there's more to come. The most important lesson in God's School of Trust would appear in an unlikely place and under unlikely conditions. We'll find out about that in the next session.

## CLOSING PRAYER

*Most Sacred Heart of Jesus, I believe in your tender love for me. I love you.*

*Most Sacred Heart of Jesus, I believe in your tender love for me. I trust in you.*

*Most Sacred Heart of Jesus, I believe in your tender love for me. I love you.*

_____

_____

_____

_____

_____

_____

# NOTES

Jesus, I Trust in You

# SESSION THREE

## THE SUFFERING SERVANT

**Step 1**

## INTRODUCTION

In our last session, we saw how God continued using his School of Trust to heal our distorted image of him. Specifically, we covered the rise of the Jansenist heresy, which attempts to distort our understanding of God's love and mercy. We saw how the Lord intervened through the revelation of the Sacred Heart to St. Margaret Mary, through the merciful moral theology of St. Alphonsus de Liguori, and through the Little Way of St. Thérèse of Lisieux. Still, his work was not over. In fact, the stage was being set for the Second Greatest Story Ever Told — in, of all places, the country of Poland.

**Step 2**

## OPENING PRAYER

*Heavenly Father,*
*we ask you for your guidance, wisdom, and insight*
*as we continue our study of your Love and Mercy.*
*Give us clear minds and attentive hearts*
*as we watch, listen, and discuss.*
*Allow us to grow closer as a group*
*and nurture the bonds of our community.*
*Fill us with your grace and draw us closer*
*to the Sacred Heart of your Son.*
*We ask all this in Jesus's name*
*and through the powerful intercession of our Blessed Mother,*
*Mary, as we pray...*

*Hail Mary, full of grace, the Lord is with thee.*
*Blessed art thou among women*
*and blessed is the fruit of thy womb, Jesus.*
*Holy Mary, Mother of God, pray for us sinners*
*now and in the hour of our death. Amen.*

**Step 3**

## VIEW VIDEO FOR EPISODE 3

# SMALL-GROUP DISCUSSION

*[Go over these questions in your small group. It's alright if your group only gets through a few of them during your discussion.]*

1. **What was your favorite part from the video? In other words, what most touched your heart or enlightened your mind?**

*- 3 Pines -*
*("Based")*

2. For the backdrop of the Second Greatest Story Ever Told, it would seem that God would choose one of the great and powerful nations of the world. Instead, he chose Poland. Yes, God chose the country that, after its glory days in the sixteenth and seventeenth centuries, soon became one of the weakest in Europe.  In fact, as we learned in the video, Poland was eventually partitioned and wiped off the map of Europe in the eighteenth century. Then, after it rose again in the twentieth century, it went on to suffer the worst casualty rate of any country during the worst war in human history (World War II) and was then essentially conquered and ruled by the Soviet Union until 1989.

*Poland*
*Jesus*
*Catholic*
*grace*

Well, that's why Poland is the perfect choice for the Second Greatest Story. After all, God himself said, "My power is made perfect in weakness" (2 Corinthians 12:9). And as St. Paul says, "But God chose what is foolish in the world to shame the wise, God chose what is weak in the world to shame the strong, God chose what is low and despised in the world, even things that are not, to bring to nothing things that are" (1 Corinthians 1:27-28). It was true in the first century, and it is true now. *So, how does the lesson of God's choice of Poland give you hope? In other words, how can you relate to Poland? For instance, do you ever feel insignificant, forgotten, overlooked, or unimportant? How, then, might God's power reach perfection in you?*

3. God chose Poland because Poland was a "suffering servant." It had been through great sufferings and hardships — partitions, invasions, death camps, brutal occupations — and yet, all the while, Poland didn't lose hope. It kept the faith. In fact, Poland's motto became, "*Semper fideles,*" meaning, "Always faithful." *How have you lived up to that motto during a time of suffering in your life? For instance, maybe it was a time when you stayed faithful to prayer when you were tempted to give it up. Or maybe it was during a time when you were tempted to give in to discouragement, but you kept trusting in God.*

## Step 4

# SMALL-GROUP DISCUSSION

4. God used Poland to save Vienna from a Muslim military invasion in 1683. Today, the threat of Islamic terrorism or terrorist acts is deeply impressed on many of our minds and hearts. *What fears do you have in an age of worldwide terrorism? How does your faith help you to deal with those fears?*

5. After his great victory at Vienna over a 200,000-man army, King Jan Sobieski of Poland declared, "*Veni, Vidi, Deus Vincit,*" meaning, "*I Came, I Saw, God Conquered.*" *Recall a time when God conquered some difficulty in your life. How did he do it? How did you thank him?*

6. The miracle on the Vistula was a modern-day David and Goliath victory. The Russians did not expect it. The world did not expect it. But the Poles did, because they believed in miracles. Unfortunately, it often seems that many Christians no longer believe in miraculous victories over great evil. *Name one specific "Goliath" problem in the world today, one that would take a miracle to defeat. Then, explain your choice and share a plan of prayer and maybe action to help defeat that evil.*

7. In this episode, we focused on ways that God used Poland to save the world. *Name one other historical miracle, blessing, or grace that affected or even changed history? What can we learn from it?*

8. This episode ended with a prophetic poem from the dark days of the partitions of Poland, a poem that announces the coming of a saint who would be a witness to hope. *Which particular saint or who among your family or friends (past or present) especially gives you hope today? What about that person gives you hope?*

> Homework: *Don't forget to read and reflect on all the questions that you don't cover during your small-group discussion!*

*[handwritten margin notes: "The Deluge 17 century" and "Sept 12 1683 Poland saved Vienna"]*

# CONCLUSION

This session's video concluded with a quote from a poem called "Into the Midst of Riotous Squabblers," written in the eighteenth century by the Polish poet Juliusz Slowacki: "Into the midst of riotous squabblers God sounds his gong; Here is the Slavic Pope, your new ruler; Make way, applaud." These words provide a prophetic foreshadowing of events that will happen a hundred years later. These events will become the Second Greatest Story Ever Told.

# CLOSING PRAYER

*Heavenly Father,*
*we thank you for the witness of the faithful people of God*
*throughout history, known and unknown,*
*who inspire us to greater faithfulness*
*even in the face of adversity and oppression.*
*Thank you for your Son, who saved them,*
*and his Mother, who watched over them with love and care.*
*Grant us the same as we go from here, desiring to live and*
*serve you in both good times and bad.*

*Glory be to the Father, and to the Son, and to the Holy Spirit,*
*as it was in the beginning, is now, and will be forever. Amen.*

## NOTES

*Jesus, I Trust in You*

# SESSION FOUR

## FAUSTINA AND THE SPREAD OF DIVINE MERCY

## Step 1 — INTRODUCTION

So far, we've learned how St. Margaret Mary helped protect God's School of Trust from the Jansenist heresy after Jesus revealed to her his Sacred Heart. Then, we saw how Poland, God's "suffering servant," helped to save the civilized world through its fidelity to its Catholic faith. Now, in this session, we'll see how Poland continues to play a vital role in God's School of Trust through a saint who will become the central catalyst for the Second Greatest Story Ever Told.

## Step 2 — OPENING PRAYER

*Jesus, give me an intellect,*
*a great intellect, for this only,*
*that I may understand you better;*
*because the better I get to know you,*
*the more ardently will I love you.*
*Jesus, I ask you for a powerful intellect,*
*that I may understand divine and lofty matters.*
*Jesus, give me a keen intellect*
*with which I will get to know your Divine Essence*
*and your indwelling, Triune life.*
*Give my intellect these capacities and aptitudes*
*by means of your special grace.*
*Amen.*

— Prayer of St. Faustina Kowalska
(*Diary*, 1474)

## Step 3 — VIEW VIDEO FOR EPISODE 4

# SMALL-GROUP DISCUSSION

*[Go over these questions in your small group. It's alright if your group only gets through a few of them during your discussion.]*

1. **What was your favorite part from the video? In other words, what most touched your heart or enlightened your mind?**

2. At the beginning of this episode, we learned that St. Thérèse of Lisieux once appeared to St. Faustina Kowalska. Now, there's something very interesting about their conversation, namely, St. Faustina's preoccupation with wanting to become a saint. In fact, she asks St. Thérèse about becoming a saint no less than *three times*: "Will I go to heaven? Will I be a saint? Will I be a saint like you, raised to the altar?" Each time, Thérèse answers, "Yes." Now, here are some questions: *What does it mean to become a saint, anyway? How strong is your desire to become a saint? In other words, taking stock of all the things you hold as important, where would you rate becoming a saint? What would it take to increase your desire for sanctity?*

3. It's interesting that St. Thérèse responds to St. Faustina that she will become a saint but adds, "But you must trust in the Lord Jesus." Well, a central part of both the Little Way of St. Thérèse and the Divine Mercy devotion is trust. In fact, St. Faustina's mission includes helping us to trust. She writes, "O doubting souls, I will draw aside for you the veils of heaven to convince you of God's goodness, so that you will no longer continue to wound with your distrust the sweetest heart of Jesus. God is love and Mercy" (*Diary*, 281). *How does St. Faustina "draw aside" for us "the veils of heaven" to convince us of God's goodness? More specifically, how has St. Faustina's mission helped you to trust more in Jesus? (If you're not very familiar with St. Faustina, then what saint, experience, or teaching has helped you to trust in Jesus?)*

4. Saint Faustina's mission seems pretty important. After all, the Lord told her, "You will prepare the world for My final coming" (*Diary*, 429). And regarding Poland, he said, "From her will come forth the spark that will prepare the world for My final coming" (*Diary*, 1732). Now, we know from Scripture that this does *not* mean that we know the day or the hour of the Lord's coming (see Mt 24:36). *So what do you think it does mean? How is it different from other apocalyptic messages that are filled with doom and gloom? How can you help prepare the world for the Lord's final coming?*

## Step 4 · SMALL-GROUP DISCUSSION

5. The Divine Mercy message and devotion brought great comfort to people who suffered the devastating effects of World War II, and it continues to comfort people amid the darkness of the modern world. After all, it's a message of consolation and hope, a message of God's compassion for those who are suffering, and a message of a Love that's more powerful than evil.

Now, of course, Divine Mercy is the message of the Gospel. It's the heart of what we read in Sacred Scripture. *Alright, but if Jesus revealed everything in the Bible (which he did), then what's the point of all the Divine Mercy Images, prayer cards, and Divine Mercy Sunday? In other words, why do you think St. Faustina's message is so important that Jesus would also give us all these different expressions of it?*

6. Consider the following facts. (1) Blessed Michael Sopocko, St. Faustina's spiritual director, confidently urged Fr. Joseph Jarzebowski, MIC, to make a highly improbable escape from Poland to the United States during World War II, carrying with him information on the Divine Mercy message and devotion — and Fr. Jarzebowski not only made it to America but spread the devotion far and wide. (2) The *very first thing* that St. John XXIII dealt with as Pope was a decree that would have forever prohibited St. Faustina's message, but he himself intervened to stop it, approving only a ban that could be lifted. (3) In her *Diary*, St. Faustina foretold the temporary ban on the Divine Mercy message and devotion and the dramatic way that God would act with power to reinstate it. (4) Six months after the ban was lifted, the bishop who had taken the initiative to get it lifted was elected Pope John Paul II.

Now, any one of these facts by itself is amazing. But all of them together is a script that only God could write. Yet this is only a small part of the Second Greatest Story Ever Told! *So, in the story up to this point, what's your favorite part? The story of the Sacred Heart? St. Alphonsus de Liguori? St. Thérèse of Lisieux? The history of Poland? (For instance, King Jan Sobieski, the Miracle on the Vistula, or Slowaski's poetic prophecy?) Or one of the points above? Why is it your favorite part?*

## SMALL-GROUP DISCUSSION

**Step 4**

7. Saint Faustina had a great love for her spiritual director, Blessed Michael Sopocko, because she saw how much he suffered to give glory to God's mercy. For instance, many times, through mystic visions, she would see him so tired yet working at his desk for the great work of Divine Mercy. She was also aware of the harsh persecutions he would have to undergo. At the same time, she often saw how Jesus looked at Fr. Sopocko with so much love and how grateful the Lord was to have such a faithful friend. Now, imagine how Jesus also looked on St. Faustina and St. John Paul II with so much love because they also poured themselves out to glorify his mercy. *Okay, so are you willing to be a faithful friend to Jesus, even if it comes with a cost? Are you willing to go out of your comfort zone to glorify God's mercy? Or, like Faustina sometimes did, do you avoid Jesus and keep a distance? Before you answer, consider the Lord's promise recorded in the* Diary *of St. Faustina: "Souls who spread the honor of My Mercy I shield through their entire lives as a tender mother her infant, and at the hour of death I will not be a Judge for them, but the Merciful Savior" (Diary, 1075). What one or two actions might you take to increase others' awareness of God's Mercy?*

8. Thanks to Fr. Joseph Jarzebowski and his brothers in the Marian Fathers of the Immaculate Conception, the Divine Mercy message and devotion has gone out to the whole world from Eden Hill, home of the National Shrine of the Divine Mercy in Stockbridge, Massachusetts. *Have you ever visited the Shrine? What was your experience? What is the main intention you would bring with you if you did go on a pilgrimage to the Shrine of Divine Mercy? Or would your pilgrimage be one of thanksgiving? For what gift of Divine Mercy would you thank God?* (To learn more about the Shrine, visit TheDivineMercy.org.)

> *Homework: Don't forget to read and reflect on all the questions that you don't cover during your small-group discussion!*

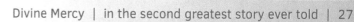

**Step 5**

## CONCLUSION

From Jesus's message to St. Faustina to the arrival of Cardinal Archbishop Karol Wojtyla, we have seen dramatic twists and turns in God's School of Trust. Next time, we'll look at the man who takes center stage in the Second Greatest Story Ever Told. In closing, let us pray with St. Faustina...

## CLOSING PRAYER

*O merciful God, You do not despise us,*
*but lavish Your graces on us continuously.*
*You make us fit to enter Your kingdom,*
*and in Your goodness You grant that human beings*
*may fill the places vacated by the ungrateful angels.*
*O God of great mercy,*
*who turned Your sacred gaze away*
*from the rebellious angels*
*and turned it upon contrite man,*
*praise and glory be to Your unfathomable mercy.*

— Prayer of St. Faustina Kowalska
(*Diary*, 1339)

*Jesus, I Trust in You*

# NOTES

# NOTES

Jesus, I Trust in You

# SESSION FIVE

## PROCLAIM THIS MESSAGE

## Step 1 — INTRODUCTION

In the last session, we looked at the powerful ways the modern message of Divine Mercy spread toward the end of St. Faustina's life and especially after her death. We saw the twists and turns in the acceptance of that message throughout the Church and how it prevailed through the efforts of the man who would go on to become both pope and saint: John Paul II.

We'll now explore the life of St. John Paul II and how this great message of Divine Mercy impacted him and his work — and how he would proclaim that message to the entire world.

## Step 2 — OPENING PRAYER

*Heavenly Father, open our minds,*
*cleanse our hearts, strengthen our bodies,*
*and quicken our souls to your Word*
*as it is revealed in our time together now.*
*We ask this in Jesus's name*
*and through the powerful intercession*
*of our Blessed Mother, Mary...*

*Hail Mary, full of grace, the Lord is with thee.*
*Blessed art thou amongst women*
*and blessed is the fruit of thy womb, Jesus.*
*Holy Mary, Mother of God, pray for us sinners*
*now and in the hour of our death.*
*Amen.*

## Step 3 — VIEW VIDEO FOR EPISODE 5

# SMALL-GROUP DISCUSSION

*[Go over these questions in your small group. It's alright if your group only gets through a few of them during your discussion.]*

1. **What was your favorite part from the video? In other words, what most touched your heart or enlightened your mind?**

2. Saint John Paul II recognized that "in the designs of providence, there are no mere coincidences." Now, as we're learning about the Second Greatest Story Ever Told, it's impossible to miss the hand of God's providence guiding and directing the events for the glory of God's mercy. *Okay, so what about in your own life? Describe something from your past where only God could have written the script. In other words, what is one event from your life where God's providence was clearly guiding and directing things?*

*Lord help me see where you are working in my life.*

3. Saint John Paul II saw the message of Divine Mercy as "doubtlessly a sign of the times" and a "special task" assigned to him by God "in the present situation of man, the Church, and the world." Alright, but what is it about our times and our present situation that points to mercy? It's the widespread evil.

—St. John Paul II's homily at beatification of St. Faustina, April 1993

God loves us so much that he doesn't want the evil in our lives and in our world to have the final word. And so, he gives us his mercy, the mercy that John Paul defines as "the specific manner in which love is revealed . . . in the face of the reality of the evil that is in the world."

Now, of course, there are great blessings in the modern world. But, again, there are also great and even unprecedented evils. *So, what are some of the specific evils of our time? In other words, what are the widespread sins that cause the great need for mercy today? Have these evils gotten better or worse since his death in 2005?*

*evil & indifference Judging Right/wrong — word of God (Guid)*

4. Saint John Paul II's encyclical letter *Dives in Misericordia*, meaning "Rich in Mercy," culminates in a call from the Pope to all of us to cry out for mercy, even with "loud cries." Specifically, we're to cry out for mercy in the name of those who don't believe there is a God and who don't know there is mercy. We're to cry out for mercy in the face of the evils discussed in the previous question. We're to cry out for mercy in the midst of our own personal sins.

*What is Divine Mercy — love greater than evil grace abound all the more pouring out in great quantite*

## Step 4 SMALL-GROUP DISCUSSION

Now, of course, the Pope isn't recommending that we belt out loud pleas for mercy while we're in a crowded church or in our homes while others are asleep. And he's certainly not advocating that we draw attention to ourselves when we pray. What he does mean is that we should pray with fervor and heartfelt compassion. *So, when was the last time you pleaded for the world with such fervor and compassion? What was it about? Why is it difficult to sometimes pray in such a way for strangers? How might you get into the habit of calling out to God for mercy with "loud cries" for the needs of the world?*

5. The Great Jubilee Year of 2000 was a year of mercy, and the mercy of that year particularly abounded on April 30, Divine Mercy Sunday. On that joyful day, Pope John Paul II canonized St. Faustina, passed the message of Divine Mercy on to the new millennium, gave an amazing homily about the gentle face of Christ depicted in the Image of Divine Mercy and the consoling prayer, "Jesus, I trust in you," declared Divine Mercy Sunday an official Feast of the Church, said it was the happiest day of his life, and fulfilled the amazing prophecy that St. Faustina recorded in her *Diary* where she actually witnessed that day. *What for you is the most amazing aspect of that marvelous day? Why? What great graces have you received on Divine Mercy Sunday? How will you prepare yourself to receive even greater graces on the next Divine Mercy Sunday?*

6. As we learned in the video, in August 2002, St. John Paul II made his last pilgrimage to Poland, and, at the dedication of the Shrine of Divine Mercy, he gave what is probably his most remarkable homily on Divine Mercy, an event that seems to have been prophesied in the *Diary* of St. Faustina. Read the stirring conclusion of that homily now:

How greatly today's world needs God's mercy. ... Today, therefore, in this Shrine, I wish solemnly to entrust the world to Divine Mercy. I do so with the burning desire that the message of God's merciful love, proclaimed here through St. Faustina, may be made known to all the peoples of the earth and fill their hearts with hope. May this message radiate from this place to our beloved homeland

# SMALL-GROUP DISCUSSION

and throughout the world. May the binding promise of the Lord Jesus be fulfilled: from here there must go forth "the spark which will prepare the world for [the Lord's] final coming." ... This spark needs to be lighted by the grace of God. This fire of mercy needs to be passed on to the world. In the mercy of God the world will find peace and mankind will find happiness!

*What are your thoughts after reading these remarkable words from the great mercy Pope? What particular statement strikes you the most and why?*

7. While St. John Paul's II's homily for the dedication of the Divine Mercy Shrine is probably his most remarkable homily on mercy, perhaps his most eloquent statement on the topic came not in words but rather in the circumstances of the very end of his life: The Pope went home to his eternal reward on the vigil of the very feast he established (Divine Mercy Sunday) shortly after receiving Holy Communion. Truly, in the designs of providence, there are no coincidences, and that event was a divine stamp on the importance of the Divine Mercy message and a reminder that God's promise is true: He shields those who spread Divine Mercy throughout their lives and their deaths will be happy ones. *grace – love – kindness*

Now, think about your own death. Think about the fact that life is short. Think about the fact that at any time your life could suddenly come to an end. *Well, in view of all that, how can your life become a story of Divine Mercy? How can your life become a witness to the most important message of our time? How can your life become a living sign and image of Divine Mercy to others? In other words, what can you do in your interactions with others, in your parish life, or in your prayer to glorify and live Divine Mercy?*

8. As we learned in the video, Pope John Paul II got to write out his last words to humanity. And in those words, he said, "How much the world needs to understand and accept Divine Mercy! ... Lord, [I] believe in you and confidently repeat to you today: Jesus, I trust in you, have mercy on us and on the whole world."

—Eucharistic celebration for the repose of the soul of Pope John Paul II

*If you could write your own final words as a message to humanity, what might they be? What would you say?* *Be kind not right*

> Homework: Don't forget to read and reflect on all the questions that you don't cover during your small-group discussion!

## Step 5 ⟩ CONCLUSION

As we close, let's think about the prayer, "Jesus, I trust in you." Through that prayer, we place our trust in Jesus Christ, who is Divine Mercy incarnate. Yet, trust is not always easy — and it's not something we do once, but again and again. As we continue the Second Greatest Story, we'll see examples of *how* we can learn to trust.

## CLOSING PRAYER

*Heavenly Father,*
*we believe that all who say the words,*
*"Jesus, I trust in you,"*
*with sincerity of heart*
*will come to experience your mercy.*
*And so we pray,*
*Jesus, I trust in you.*
*Jesus, I trust in you.*
*Jesus, I trust in you.*
*Amen.*

*Jesus, I Trust in You*

*Jesus I trust in You!*

## NOTES

What is Divine Mercy — grace abounded all the more
closeness to God.
Mercy second word for Love

host light spread to the whole world.
profound peace —
Bless those infinite mercy.
spirit engulfed in love.
Divine Mercy Sunday — 1 2nd Sunday Easter

joy — accomplished mission
love more powerful than evil.
S M
Compassion —
in mercy — find peace.
Binding promise — grace
spark — Divine Mercy — merciful love.
1931     relief first love
initiator of love
Christ has entered our time

undoing — Jansenism.

# NOTES

_____

_____

_____

_____

_____

_____

_____

_____

_____

_____

_____

_____

_____

_____

_____

_____

_____

_____

Jesus, I Trust in You

# SESSION SIX

## FATIMA

# SESSION 6 〉 FATIMA

Step **1**

## INTRODUCTION

In the last session, we saw the culmination of God's School of Trust in the mission of St. John Paul II and the message of Divine Mercy he proclaimed to the world. Now we'll look at others who heralded that same work through their lives and efforts.

Step **2**

## OPENING PRAYER

> *Most Holy Trinity —*
> *Father, Son, and Holy Spirit —*
> *I adore Thee profoundly.*
> *I offer Thee the most precious Body, Blood, Soul,*
> *and Divinity of Jesus Christ,*
> *present in all the tabernacles of the world,*
> *in reparation for the outrages, sacrileges,*
> *and indifferences whereby He is offended.*
> *And through the infinite merits*
> *of His Most Sacred Heart*
> *and the Immaculate Heart of Mary,*
> *I beg of Thee the conversion of poor sinners.*
>
> —Prayer of Fatima

Step **3**

## VIEW VIDEO FOR EPISODE 6

# SMALL-GROUP DISCUSSION

*[Go over these questions in your small group. It's alright if your group only gets through a few of them during your discussion.]*

1. **What was your favorite part from the video? In other words, what most touched your heart or enlightened your mind?**

2. Poor Pope Benedict XV! He became pope just a month after the start of the worst war in history up to that time. He worked for peace and fervently prayed for peace, but nothing seemed to be working; the war ground on, taking millions of lives and devastating Europe. Finally, with the whole Church, Pope Benedict prayed a novena to Mary, the Mother of God, and on May 13, 1917, she appeared to three shepherd children in Fatima on the 8th day of the novena. Of course, Benedict XV wouldn't have known about this until much later, if at all. (The apparitions of Fatima were not approved by the Church until 1930.) *When in your life have you fervently prayed for something, thought your prayers weren't answered, and then discovered after the fact that God did answer your prayers? Or have you ever prayed for something and had your prayers answered in a way that surprised you or that you did not expect?*

3. The "First Secret" of Fatima consisted of a vision of hell that had a profound effect on the three children. Read and reflect on Lucia's description of that vision:

> Our Lady showed us a great sea of fire which seemed to be under the earth. Plunged in this fire were demons and souls in human form, like transparent burning embers, all blackened or burnished bronze, floating about in the conflagration, now raised into the air by the flames that issued from within themselves together with great clouds of smoke, now falling back on every side like sparks in a huge fire, without weight or equilibrium, and amid shrieks and groans of pain and despair, which horrified us and made us tremble with fear. The demons could be distinguished by their terrifying and repellent likeness to frightful and unknown animals, all black and transparent. This vision lasted but an instant. How can we ever be grateful enough to our kind heavenly Mother, who had already prepared us by promising, in the first apparition, to take us to heaven? Otherwise, I think we would have died of fear and terror.

*What is your reaction to this description? How do you feel after reading it? Afraid? Prayerful? More determined to avoid hell? More determined to help others avoid that place of unending misery? What action can you take in response to this vision?*

## Step 4 — SMALL-GROUP DISCUSSION

4. The Second Secret of Fatima foretold terrible wars, famine, and harsh persecution of the Church, all of which came to pass. However, it could have been prevented if Our Lady's message had been heeded. Imagine that: no World War II, no Nazi or Soviet domination, no concentration camps, no major famines, no mass rapes, no orphan crises, no major loss of faith to atheism. If people only knew in 1917 the full extent of the horrors that could have been prevented, as we do today, the message of Fatima surely would have been heeded by all! But they did know it. Our Lady of Fatima had warned them; she foretold what would happen.

Now we find ourselves in a great time of mercy, a time when, as we learned in the previous episode, we're being asked to cry out to God for mercy. Why? Because without Divine Mercy, there will be Divine Justice and a great punishment for humanity's many sins, sins that are much worse and more extensive than those that led to World War I and II. But this time, the warning doesn't come through three shepherd children. Rather, it comes through three popes: John Paul II, Benedict XVI, and Francis, all of whom have urged the Church to heed the present time of mercy. *How will you take this urgent message of mercy to heart? What are you going to do with it now that you've heard it? How are you going to live it?*

5. The Third Secret of Fatima paints a symbolic picture of the suffering of the Church amid the "wars, famine, and persecution" that Mary had warned about. It's a graphic image of pain, sorrow, corpses, and killing. Apparently, Our Lady of Fatima, who also showed the children a terrible vision of hell, is not afraid to emphasize the reality of suffering caused by sin. Perhaps that's because, from her vantage point of heaven, she sees all the offenses against God in great detail, and it breaks her Immaculate Heart. Also, she sees how so many of her children don't let her into their hearts and don't accept her tender care. Well, through the first Saturday devotion, which is part of the message of Fatima, we're essentially called to comfort our Blessed Mother by spending time with her. This makes "reparation" for sins committed. *Have you ever spent time with Mary for the purpose of consoling her Immaculate Heart? If so, what was that like? How have you experienced her giving consolation to your heart?*

## SMALL-GROUP DISCUSSION

**6.** In the video, I shared that when my father first heard the story of Our Lady of Fatima and the Miracle of the Sun, he responded by saying, "If people heard that, they'd believe!" *What specific part of what we've covered in* Divine Mercy in the Second Greatest Story Ever Told *do you think might convince someone to believe in God, who is Love and Mercy itself? For instance, was it something having to do with Saints Margaret Mary, Faustina Kowalska, John Paul II, another part of the Fatima messages, or something else we've covered?*

**7.** Some 70,000 people saw the Miracle of the Sun at Fatima, and they surely told others about it. *Have you ever witnessed something you consider a miracle or an extraordinary grace? What was it?*

**8.** Normally, God doesn't work spectacular miracles for the world to see as he did at Fatima. However, he does often speak to us in our daily lives in subtle but real ways. *Can you think of a time recently when God gave you a "sign" or evidence of his power, presence, or providence in your life? For instance, describe a time when you felt a deep peace that seemed to come out of nowhere in the midst of a distressing situation. Or share a time when you received an inspiration or light in the midst of a moment when you were confused about a problem. Or explain a time when you were given clear direction, a sign of confirmation, or courage regarding a course of action.*

> *Homework: Don't forget to read and reflect on all the questions that you don't cover during your small-group discussion!*

## Step 5 | CONCLUSION

As remarkable as the events at Fatima were and still are, they were only one part of God's plan to impact the world. In our next session, we'll take another step into the astonishing unfolding of the Second Greatest Story Ever Told.

## CLOSING PRAYER

*My God,*
*I believe, I adore, I hope, and I love Thee!*
*I ask pardon for those who do not believe,*
*do not adore, do not hope, and do not love Thee. ...*
*O, My Jesus,*
*forgive us our sins,*
*save us from the fires of Hell,*
*lead all souls to Heaven,*
*especially those in most need of Thy mercy.*

—Prayer of Fatima

*Jesus, I Trust in You*

## NOTES

The move 1950 Fatimelier

# NOTES

# SESSION SEVEN

## THE SECRET OF DIVINE MERCY

### Step 1 — INTRODUCTION

In our last session, we saw the miraculous drama of Fatima play out against a world engulfed in war. We'll now see how other dramatic events bring together the power of Divine Mercy in the Second Greatest Story Ever Told.

### Step 2 — OPENING PRAYER

> *Heavenly Father,*
> *we echo the words of St. John Paul the Great,*
> *who called out to Mary in his time of need,*
> *and recognized that any suffering in his life*
> *was an opportunity for you*
> *to provide special graces —*
> *not only for him, but for the entire Church.*
> *We ask now for the grace to understand*
> *and live out your mercy to all those around us,*
> *even those who would attempt to do us harm.*
> *We ask all this in Jesus's name. Amen.*
>
> —Adapted from words of Pope John Paul II,
> spoken shortly after the events of May 13, 1981

### Step 3 — VIEW VIDEO FOR EPISODE 7

# SMALL-GROUP DISCUSSION

*[Go over these questions in your small group. It's alright if your group only gets through a few of them during your discussion.]*

1. **What was your favorite part from the video? In other words, what most touched your heart or enlightened your mind?**

2. The Third Secret of Our Lady of Fatima came true ... but not completely. The "bishop dressed in white," the Pope, was indeed shot — but he did not die. Why not? Well, because as the future Pope Benedict XVI put it, "The future is not in fact unchangeably set, ... [it] is in no way a film preview of a future in which nothing can be changed." Moreover, he said that the whole point of the vision was to bring freedom onto the scene, to steer it in a positive direction, and to mobilize the forces of change in the right direction. In short, prayer can change things. Grace and mercy can work miracles.

Sometimes you may be tempted to write people off, including yourself, thinking that they or their situation (or you and your situation) will never change for the better. Well, that is the definition of despair. But hope says differently. Hope says that God's grace can bring about change in a positive direction — though it leaves God room to bring it about in his way and in his time. *So, where could you use this kind of hope in your life? In other words, where do you need the good news that God's grace can change any situation or problem?*

3. "I know I was aiming right. I know that the bullet was a killer. So why aren't you dead?" According to St. John Paul II's longtime personal secretary and friend, Stanislaus Dziwisz, those words of the Pope's would-be assassin had a profound effect on the Pope. He said that John Paul "carried [those words] around with him for years, pondering [them] over and over again." Those words were a confirmation for the Pope that the Lord had spared his life through the intercession of Our Lady, and they surely deepened his gratitude for the gift of his life. *What words or event in your life might you ponder over and over again to deepen your gratitude to God for his goodness to you?*

## SMALL-GROUP DISCUSSION

4. Saint John Paul II said five days after being attacked, "I am praying for the brother who wounded me and whom I sincerely forgive." Now, sometimes in the news, to the amazement of our secular society, Christians share that they forgive the killers of one of their loved ones. Of course, as Christians we're called to forgive our enemies and those who hurt us, yet, at the same time, Christians sometimes say, "I could never do that. If that happened to me or my family, I could never forgive that person." *How do we become the kind of people who would be ready to forgive those who hurt us or our family members? For instance, how might we begin to pray in order to grow in having a spirit of forgiveness? What little things can we begin to forgive more readily in preparation to forgive the bigger things?*

5. Even before he read the Third Secret of Fatima about "the bishop dressed in white," Pope John Paul II was convinced that Our Lady of Fatima had spared his life. Why? Well, the May 13th anniversary of the first apparition of Fatima had a lot to do with it. For him, it was not a mere coincidence. The anniversary date spoke to him. *Can you think of a time in your life when God spoke to you through an anniversary or a significant date? What was the date, and what do you think God was saying to you through it?*

6. The secret of Divine Mercy is the power of God's love to bring not only good out of evil but an even greater good out of evil. It's the truth that should prevent us from ever despairing, because no matter how great the darkness of our sins, God can still bring not just good but an even greater good *if* we turn away from sin and place our trust in him. *Share one time in your life when God brought not only good but an even greater good out of some evil or seemingly hopeless situation.*

**Step 4**

# SMALL-GROUP DISCUSSION

7. The secret of Divine Mercy was at work in the midst of the evils and horrors of the Second World War and the brutality of the Soviet Union. Of course, God tried to prevent all those evils in the first place by sending Our Lady of Fatima to try to inspire people to convert and pray. But apparently not enough people were inspired. Nevertheless, once the evils came, God brought good out of them through the blood of the martyrs, and it's their blood that gives us the present time of mercy in the Church. *What sacrifices or suffering have you undergone to help bring about a greater good for another person? Or what sufferings has someone else accepted out of love for you to bring a greater good in your life?*

8. Saint John Paul II was not killed by an assassin's bullet, but he became a martyr nonetheless through the way he bore illness and old age as he carried the weight of the world for twenty-six long years as pope. In fact, according to papal biographer George Weigel, John Paul's last months and painful death were "his last and greatest encyclical," which showed us how to suffer with love for others in union with Christ. *How has St. John Paul II's example of suffering helped you? Which crosses in your life will you try to bear with more love? For whom or for what will you offer them?*

> *Homework: Don't forget to read and reflect on all the questions that you don't cover during your small-group discussion!*

## Step 5

## CONCLUSION

There's a lot to think about in today's session. May each one of us take a little extra time to ponder the wonder of Fatima and the remarkable events surrounding St. John Paul II's early days as pope. Now, there's still a lot more to come with St. John Paul II and the unfolding work of God's mercy over the past century.

## CLOSING PRAYER

*Heavenly Father,*
*just as we have been disobedient to you,*
*we now receive mercy because you are full of mercy,*
*even toward those who have rejected you.*
*How can we fathom the depths*
*of your riches and wisdom and knowledge?*
*Your ways truly are unsearchable*
*and your judgments are beyond our scrutiny.*
*We cannot know your mind.*
*We cannot presume to question your ways.*
*Your gifts to us are more than we can ever repay.*
*For from you and through you and to you*
*are ascribed all things.*
*To you be glory for ever.*
  *Amen.*

— Adapted from Romans 11:30-36

*Jesus, I Trust in You*

# NOTES

## NOTES

Jesus, I Trust in You

# SESSION EIGHT

## GOD'S MASTER PLAN

## Step 1 · INTRODUCTION

Over the past few sessions, we've covered the historical tapestry of God's mercy, an interweaving of the events at Fatima, the life of St. Faustina Kowalska, the attempted assassination of Pope John Paul II, the sacrifices and suffering of the nation of Poland, and so much more. Now, we'll look more closely at John Paul's pivotal role in international events that once again show us God's amazing mercy at work.

## Step 2 · OPENING PRAYER

*Hail Mary,*
*beloved Daughter of the Eternal Father!*
*Hail Mary, admirable Mother of the Son!*
*Hail Mary, faithful spouse of the Holy Spirit! ...*
*Destroy in us all that may be displeasing to God;*
*place and cultivate in us everything that is pleasing to you.*
*May the light of your faith*
*dispel the darkness of our minds;*
*may your profound humility take the place of our pride;*
*may your sublime contemplation*
*check the distractions of our wandering imaginations.*
*Do all that you do in our souls,*
*so that you alone may fully glorify Jesus in us*
*for time and eternity.*
*Amen.*

— Adapted from a Marian prayer of St. Louis de Montfort

## Step 3 · VIEW VIDEO FOR EPISODE 8

# SMALL-GROUP DISCUSSION

*[Go over these questions in your small group. It's alright if your group only gets through a few of them during your discussion.]*

1. **What was your favorite part from the video? In other words, what most touched your heart or enlightened your mind?**

2. Saint John Paul II consecrated himself totally to Jesus through Mary at a young age, and then he took his consecration very seriously. For instance, he renewed it every day, wrote the consecration prayer "*totus tuus*" ("totally yours") at the top of many of his handwritten pages, and prayed brief prayers of entrustment to Jesus through Mary throughout the day. **What are your favorite brief prayers that you try to pray in the midst of your day?**

3. As an Archbishop, Karol Wojtyla chose as his episcopal coat of arms a golden cross with the letter "M" on the lower right, which represents the Gospel of John 19:26-27. Then, at the bottom of the coat of arms, he chose as his motto "*totus tuus.*" **If you were to make a coat of arms for yourself, what would it look like? How would it reflect the people or things most important to you? If you were to choose a motto, what would it be?**

4. Again, St. John Paul II consecrated himself to Jesus through Mary at a young age, and it had a profound effect on his life. In fact, he called his consecration "a decisive turning point" in his life. **What does it mean for you (or what would it mean for you) to consecrate yourself totally to Jesus through Mary?**

5. Pope John Paul II's first two attempts at consecrating the world and Russia to Mary's Immaculate Heart were not completely successful. One reason had to do with his physical health. The other had to do with getting the invitations out too late. (And maybe also the people he was trying to invite were not as interested in it as he was.) Nevertheless, the Pope didn't give up. In fact, for the third time, he made sure the invitations went out on time, and he studied the situation even more carefully. **Have you ever wanted to do some project or good work for the Lord and his people but didn't do it or complete it because obstacles arose? What was it? Is it possible to somehow try it again, maybe by using a different strategy or modifying the project itself so it can be a success? What might you do?**

## SMALL-GROUP DISCUSSION

6. On its surface, it seems that St. John Paul II's visit to Fatima, Portugal, on May 13, 1982 was a failure. After all, it was there in Portugal that he had wanted to consecrate Russia and the whole world to Mary's Immaculate Heart in union with all the bishops. But it didn't work out because, again, the invitations went out too late. Despite that failure, there was at least one significant victory: The Pope gave to the world what is possibly his most insightful message about Marian consecration, a message in which he tells us what it essentially means. Specifically, he said, "Consecrating ourselves to Mary means to accept her help to offer ourselves and the whole of mankind to he who is holy," to he who is "Love itself, merciful Love." According to the Pope, Marian consecration means "drawing near, through the Mother's intercession to the very Fountain of Life that sprang from Golgotha," the "Fountain of Merciful Love," as he called it later. So, we need Mary's help to offer ourselves to Merciful Love. We need her prayers to draw near to Jesus' pierced side, the Fountain of Mercy. *Well, how have you experienced this motherly help to accept God's mercy in the past? Or what specific graces of mercy would you like her help accepting in the future?*

7. Less than seven months after St. John Paul II successfully consecrated Russia and the world in union with the bishops of the world, Blessed Jerzy Popieluszko, the famous chaplain of the Solidarity Labor Union, was martyred by Soviet secret police. His martyrdom then galvanized the supporters of Solidarity and eventually helped inspire them to take bold action, action that quickly brought down Communism in Poland, the rest of Europe, and finally in Russia itself.

Now, at the time of Popieluszko's death, many might have seen his death not as a victory for Solidarity but rather for the Soviets. However, as we now know, by killing Popieluszko, the Soviets basically sealed their own fate. So it is in the Christian life: The acceptance of suffering and death in faith leads to the glory of the Resurrection. *Now, can you think of a dying in your own life (for instance, a failure or a loss) that later led to life and the glory of God?*

## SMALL-GROUP DISCUSSION

8. God's master plan seems to be for the whole Church to recognize and make the connection between the Immaculate Heart of Mary and the Sacred Heart of Jesus. In other words, in all hearts, he wants there to be devotion to the Immaculate Heart of Mary alongside devotion to the Sacred Heart of Jesus.

Now, the Lord had wanted to make this connection for the world through the Triumph of the Immaculate Heart that would have resulted had Russia been consecrated back in 1917. But that didn't work out (humanity didn't adequately respond), so God's glorious "Plan B" kicked in, a plan that raised up from the ashes of World War II and Communism a man who unites in himself the Immaculate Heart and the Sacred Heart as a triumph of Divine Mercy, namely, St. John Paul II. Also, this was a plan that now gives us a time of mercy from the blood of more martyrs than all centuries combined. *Alright, so having heard much of the Second Greatest Story Ever Told, in your own words, try to explain the connection between the Immaculate Heart of Mary and the Sacred Heart of Jesus in this time of mercy. In other words, can you describe how the Triumph of Mary's Immaculate Heart is really the Triumph of Divine Mercy?*

*Homework: Don't forget to read and reflect on all the questions that you don't cover during your small-group discussion!*

**Step 5**

## CONCLUSION

We've seen yet again how the setbacks and accomplishments of the past 100 years have brought clarity and fulfillment to the prophetic message of Fatima. Among the many lessons for us to learn, we can see how the people of God have played key roles in fulfilling the purposes of God. And we'll see a dramatic example of that truth in our next session.

## CLOSING PRAYER

*I belong totally to you, Mother of God,*
*and all that I have is yours.*
*I take you for my all.*
*O Mary, give me your heart.*

— Adapted from one of
Karol Wojtyla's favorite prayers

*impatience — my time*
*our first sin not trusting.*
*- 40 days suffering + angel helping*
*40 years*
*master plan.*
*faith — that you a trust that mean underneath*
*loved,*

*Jesus, I Trust in You*

## NOTES

Grace & Peace
- consecration - Morning Glory 33
- immaculate heart of Mary
  sacred heart of Jesus.
collapse of communism 1984 - Soviet Union
  Power of Merciful Love.
- light of hope

Faustina - Kolbe -
  Mary - Divine Mercy
Pope Marian / Mercy.

Paul Kengor Pope & President.
  Kendor.

An SPM
Archbishop synod

## NOTES

Jesus, I Trust in You

# SESSION NINE

## MARY'S KNIGHT

## Step 1 — INTRODUCTION

In the mix of people and events surrounding the Second Greatest Story Ever Told, it's important for us to recognize one person we've hardly mentioned, a person who influenced St. John Paul II and countless others in his passion for the glory of God and his amazing mercy.

## Step 2 — OPENING PRAYER

*Heavenly Father,*
*we give thanks for your abundant love and mercy.*
*Please give us the grace to share your love and mercy*
*with everyone around us, friend or adversary,*
*just as many of your children*
*who came before us have done.*
*We ask this all in Jesus's name*
*and through the powerful intercession*
*of Our Blessed Mother, Mary...*

*Hail Mary, full of grace, the Lord is with thee.*
*Blessed art thou among women*
*and blessed is the fruit of thy womb, Jesus.*
*Holy Mary, Mother of God, pray for us sinners*
*now and in the hour of our death. Amen.*

## Step 3 — VIEW VIDEO FOR EPISODE 9

# SMALL-GROUP DISCUSSION

*[Go over these questions in your small group. It's alright if your group only gets through a few of them during your discussion.]*

1. **What was your favorite part from the video? In other words, what most touched your heart or enlightened your mind?**

2. In the video, I shared that when I first saw a photo of St. Maximilian Kolbe, I didn't like him, because he looked so stern and intense. Later, I discovered that his was a beautiful intensity, an intensity of love. Now, there are many people we interact with in our day-to-day lives about whom we know the obvious (teacher, police officer, mother, father, wife) or we may even judge them based on their appearance. But then, later, we discover their beautiful hearts. *Now, recall an acquaintance only known through job or function (janitor, cafeteria worker) until you learned about his or her life burdens and faith in God. How did you learn about the life and faith of that person? How did you change your perception of him or her? What helps you now to see beyond the functions, jobs, or appearances of people around you?*

3. The young Kolbe was like a fire hose with the nozzle on the mist setting. In other words, he had a lot of intensity, but he didn't exactly know where to direct it and ended up going off in a thousand different directions. *Have you ever felt that you were going off in a thousand directions without a single purpose? What experience or insight helped tighten the nozzle so that you became more focused? In other words, what has tightened your focus, giving you purpose and direction in life? If this study and group experience has helped you with a specific change in your focus, purpose, or direction, please share how it has done so.*

4. The single idea that most tightened the nozzle for St. Maximilian Kolbe, directing his intensity to a single goal, was probably this one: *a total consecration to Jesus through Mary is the quickest and easiest way to become a saint.* After all, Kolbe wanted to give the greatest possible glory to God, and what better way to give him glory than by becoming a saint? And what's better: one saint or ten saints, ten saints or a thousand saints? For Kolbe, being an apostle of Marian consecration was how he believed he could win the whole world for God, under the generalship of Mary Immaculate, as quickly as possible. *What impression does Kolbe's bold goal make on you? How have you been an apostle of Marian consecration in the past? How might you be one in the future?*

## SMALL-GROUP DISCUSSION

5. Saint Maximilian Kolbe continually asked, "How can I give the greatest possible glory to God?" *What's the difference between desiring to give glory to God versus giving God the greatest possible glory? How might you give the greatest possible glory to God?*

6. The essence of Kolbe's army for Mary Immaculate is "to be an instrument in her Immaculate hands" — and that is a powerful statement. It's like this: Mary is the mother of all humanity, and she sees the sins and suffering of each and every one of her children, which breaks her heart. Of course, she longs to help them, and she does so through her prayers, but she also wants us to help her. Specifically, she's looking for people who will give her permission to use them as living instruments in her hands to help her children — that is what it means to be an instrument in Mary's hands. *Have you ever experienced someone as an instrument of your love to your child, your parent, another relative, or to a friend? Perhaps it was an instance where you had difficulty in that relationship. Perhaps it was a time when you couldn't get through to your loved one, but this other person did. Share what happened when the other person helped. How did you feel about their help? Were you grateful? Consider Mary's gratitude to those who offer themselves as instruments for her to help her children. She is our Immaculate Mother asking for our help for the sake of all her children. How will you say yes to being her instrument?*

## SMALL-GROUP DISCUSSION

7. Saying yes to being an instrument in Mary's hands is not only a gift to our spiritual mother, Mary, it's also a gift to our heavenly Father. After all, because of the wound of original sin that makes us doubt his goodness, our heavenly Father has an uphill battle of trying to get people to trust in him. Of course, he sent his Son to teach us his mercy, but because his Son, Jesus, is also God, people tend to fear Jesus, too! That is where Mary comes in. She's not God, but she's an instrument of God's mercy, leading us to Jesus. She's not the source of mercy — Jesus is the source of mercy — but she's an instrument of mercy, leading us to that source. But because of various prejudices and misunderstandings, people even avoid that most tender of mothers!

So, that's where you come in. When you offer yourself to Mary as an instrument in her hands, she uses you to bring people to the Heart of her Son. *Now, describe a time when you were an instrument of such mercy, particularly to someone who wanted nothing to do with God. Why do you think they listened to you? How did that encounter impact you?*

8. Kolbe's Knights of Niepokalanow, who were part of the largest monastery in the world, truly conquered all of Poland for Mary Immaculate and prepared Poland for World War II. They brought the whole country close to Mary's Immaculate Heart, so she could comfort them as they would go through their trial by fire. In fact, just as Mary was a consolation to her Son, Jesus, as he was dying on the Cross, so she also gave consolation to the Poles as they went through their own suffering during the war. This is important because it shows us that Marian consecration isn't just about being an instrument in Mary's hands so she can comfort others. She also wants to comfort you. She is your mother, and she wants you to say yes to her, so she can be that tender, motherly presence in your life. *Share a time when you or a friend were suffering greatly and Mary brought you or your friend great comfort. Or, simply describe a time when you experienced Mary as your tender mother.*

> *Homework: Don't forget to read and reflect on all the questions that you don't cover during your small-group discussion!*

## CONCLUSION

The intense love of St. Maximilian Kolbe is inspiring to us now, as it was also inspiring to St. John Paul II. Both men are now saints. So, we might conclude that St. Louis de Montfort's claim that Mary is the quickest, easiest, and surest means to becoming a saint has some validity. But with so many aspects to the Second Greatest Story Ever Told, how can we take what we've learned and live it in our lives? That's what we'll consider next time.

## CLOSING PRAYER

*Almighty and Eternal God,*
*you gave us in the person of St. Maximilian Kolbe*
*an example of true devotion to the Immaculate Mother*
*of our Savior and of unselfish love for our neighbor.*
*Grant, we beseech you, through his intercession,*
*that we may grow in our understanding*
*and love of the Immaculata;*
*that we may recognize her presence, her voice, her love,*
*and her power with us and be filled with an ardent desire*
*and will to fulfill her will*
*[which is perfectly united with God's will] in every detail,*
*and thus become sharers and true instruments*
*of her most perfect response to you,*
*in the Holy Spirit through Christ our Lord.*
*Amen.*

— Prayer from the Militia of the Immaculata

*(God wound.) - so Mary averts - to head*

*Distrust Him —                    distorted image*

*Restore   image of God*

*old lie*

*new woman Mary heal motherhood*

*Mary helps ↳ school of trust*

*lead us to the source of mercy Jesus.*

*Jesus, I Trust in You*

# NOTES

## NOTES

Jesus, I Trust in You

# SESSION TEN

## THE FINAL QUESTION

## Step 1 INTRODUCTION

As we wrap up the Second Greatest Story Ever Told, we'll now look at how that great story can continue with *our* stories.

## Step 2 OPENING PRAYER

*Heavenly Father,*
*please open our hearts, minds, and souls*
*to the truth of your Divine Mercy.*
*Help us to take to heart all that we're learning*
*and experiencing about your mercy,*
*so it may transform our lives*
*and make us better instruments of mercy to others.*
*We ask all this in Jesus's name*
*and through the powerful intercession*
*of Our Blessed Mother, Mary...*

*Hail Mary, full of grace, the Lord is with thee.*
*Blessed art thou among women*
*and blessed is the fruit of thy womb, Jesus.*
*Holy Mary, Mother of God, pray for us sinners*
*now and in the hour of our death. Amen.*

## Step 3 VIEW VIDEO FOR EPISODE 10

# SMALL-GROUP DISCUSSION

Step 4

*[Go over these questions in your small group. It's alright if your group only gets through a few of them during your discussion.]*

1. **What was your favorite part from the video? In other words, what most touched your heart or enlightened your mind?**

2. Pope Francis, inspired by St. John Paul II, believes that *now is the time of mercy.* Reflect on his powerful words:

> [L]isten to the voice of the Spirit that speaks to the whole Church in this our time, which is in fact, the time of mercy. I am certain of this. . . . We have been living in the time of mercy for 30 or more years, up to now. It is the time of mercy in the whole Church. It was instituted by [St.] John Paul II. He had the "intuition" that this was the time of mercy.
>
> —Pope Francis to the parish priests of the diocese of Rome, March 2014

*What do these words mean for you? How do they make you feel? What is your response?*

3. In the video, I shared my own personal story, hoping that it would help you make the Second Greatest Story your story. I shared about how, when I was in college, I didn't think I could be like the holy students I saw all around me or like the saints I learned about in my theology classes. I shared about how I found hope that I really and truly could become a saint, despite my great weakness, by giving my life totally to Jesus through Mary, the "quickest and easiest" way to holiness. I shared how I became discouraged and disappointed when the "warm fuzzies" of that consecration wore off, and how I believed that Mary had rejected me. I shared about how my image of Mary was one that made me want to keep my distance. *What part of all this most resonates with you? For instance, when have you felt that you could not live up to the lives of the saints? Or when has discouragement caused you to feel rejected by Mary or one of the saints to whom you have devotion? Can you share any part of those experiences? How might you look at those experiences differently now?*

## SMALL-GROUP DISCUSSION

4. Saint Maximilian Kolbe's testimony helped heal my devotion to Mary, especially the following two citations:

> *"My dear, dear brothers, our dear little, little mother, the Immaculate Mary can do anything for us. We are her children. Turn to her. She will overcome anything."*
>
> *—A Man for Others*, pg. 66

> *"Sometimes, my dear ones, the thought, a sad longing, as if a plea or a complaint may occur to you, "Does the Immaculata still love me?" Most beloved children! I tell you all and each one individually in her name, mark that, in her name! She loves every one of you. She loves you very much and at every moment with no exception. This I repeat for you in her name."*
>
> *—The Kolbe Reader* (Libertyville, IL: Franciscan Mayrtown Press, 1987, pg. 96)

*What part of St. Maximilian Kolbe's words most reassure you of Mary's love for you personally? Why? What new insight do they provide for you, if any?*

5. Saint John Paul II taught that Mary is the one who brings us to the "Fountain of Mercy," the pierced side of Jesus. She's the one whose powerful prayers help us to trust in Divine Mercy. She's the one who helps us to believe that God loves us not because of what we do but because of what God has done for us and that God loves us because he's good, not because we are. She helps us understand that we need not hide from God out of fear. She helps us realize that Jesus did not come for the righteous but for sinners and that it's our misery that attracts him and that the more weak, broken, and sinful we are, the more his merciful Heart goes out to us. She helps us realize that the greater the sinner, the greater right he has to God's mercy. She's the one who helps us feel contrition and sorrow for our sins.

Now, your understanding of God's mercy may have grown or deepened through this program. *What is your response to those changes? Do you want to ask Mary for more help in coming to better understand and accept God's love for you? What can you do to allow her to give you that help?*

# SMALL-GROUP DISCUSSION

Step 4

**6.** In the video, I shared how my staff and I have received countless emails, phone calls, and letters from people sharing the powerful ways that Mary has worked in their lives through the consecration. ***Do you know of any powerful stories related to Marian consecration? Or can you share a story or testimony about Marian consecration that encouraged you or caused you to want to learn more about it?***

**7.** I concluded the video by making three recommendations. Let's look at them again:

(1) *Make, renew, and spread Marian consecration.* So, if you haven't made your consecration, then make it! If you have made it, then renew it — and not just every year but *every day.* And then, like St. Maximilian Kolbe, spread it! I mean, if Marian consecration is the quickest, easiest, and surest way to become a saint, then we've got to tell everybody!

(2) *Experience Divine Mercy.* Now, as we've already learned, Mary is the best help for bringing us to experience the merciful love of her Son, which is why my first recommendation was to make the consecration. But what else helps us to experience Divine Mercy? Of course, becoming more deeply aware of our sins and going to Confession more frequently helps us to experience Divine Mercy. I mean, if we don't realize we're sinners, Divine Mercy doesn't make sense! Also, along with Mass, Confession, and the reading of Sacred Scripture, I encourage you to get to know more deeply the Divine Mercy message and devotion that comes to us through St. Faustina. For instance, read her *Diary* and learn more about Divine Mercy Sunday, the Image of Divine Mercy, the Novena, Chaplet, and Hour of Great Mercy. All of that can help you to better experience Divine Mercy when you turn to prayer, the Sacraments, and Sacred Scripture.

(3) *Live Divine Mercy.* Now, living Divine Mercy means being merciful to others in deed, word, and prayer. It means forgiving those who have hurt us and letting go of resentment, bitterness, and hate. It means crying out for mercy on ourselves, our families, our society, and on the whole world, for instance, by praying the Chaplet of Divine Mercy.

***What changes will you have to make to follow these recommendations? Will it be difficult for you to make such changes? What help might you ask of this group with whom you have shared so much, so that you can follow these recommendations, even the most difficult?***

## SMALL-GROUP DISCUSSION

8. Throughout this series, we've heard all about what I believe is the greatest story after Sacred Scripture, the Second Greatest Story Ever Told. Now, it's certainly not great because of the teller, and I apologize for my many shortcomings in telling it. But despite my weaknesses, I knew it had to be told! I mean, the story surrounding the life of St. John Paul II, which includes the amazing history of Poland, the mission of St. Faustina Kowalska, St. Maximilian Kolbe, and the children of Fatima is truly amazing, and I hope you now agree that it really is the Second Greatest Story Ever Told.

But why did God give us such an incredible story right now in our time? I believe he gave it to try to convince us of something that may seem too good to be true. Again, it's the good news that *now is the time of mercy*. And the whole story, I believe, is meant to convince us of that. I hope it has convinced you and that you've been encouraged by the good news of this time of mercy. *So what difference is this good news going to make in your life? How will you invite others to believe in and live this good news of God's mercy?*

> *Homework: Don't forget to read and reflect on all the questions that you don't cover during your small-group discussion!*

## CONCLUSION

Now that we've participated in this entire series *Divine Mercy in the Second Greatest Story Ever Told* and have been encouraged to make its story our own, one question remains: *Will we, in fact, make it our own?* In other words, will we consecrate ourselves to Jesus through Mary and encourage others to do so as well? Will we strive to experience Divine Mercy? And will we put mercy into action in our daily lives? (To learn more, visit MarianMissionaries.org.) Now, before the Closing Prayer, take a time of silence to speak with God about this.

*Jesus, I Trust in You*

# CLOSING PRAYER

*(After a time of silence.)*
*Heavenly Father, thank you for the great time of mercy*
*you are giving to the Church and the world.*
*Lord, please fill us with the fire of your Holy Spirit.*
*Help us to receive your love deeply into our hearts.*
*Give us the grace to trust in your mercy even more.*
*Make us powerful instruments of mercy*
*in the hands of our Immaculate Mother, Mary.*

*Blessed Mother, please bring us to the pierced side of Jesus, the*
*Fountain of Mercy, and teach us to pray...*

*O Blood and Water, which gushed forth from the Heart of Jesus as*
*a fountain of mercy for us, I trust in you.*

*O Blood and Water, which gushed forth from the Heart of Jesus as*
*a fountain of mercy for us, I trust in you.*

*O Blood and Water, which gushed forth from the Heart of Jesus as*
*a fountain of mercy for us, I trust in you. Amen.*

# NOTES

# APPENDIX

## INFORMATION FOR SMALL-GROUP LEADERS

# SMALL-GROUP DYNAMICS AND SEVEN TIPS FOR MANAGING THEM

Each person is an unrepeatable, unfathomable mystery that should trigger our sense of wonder. Even more so then, a whole group of persons who gather together in Christ is a mystery worthy of our contemplation and awe. What depth of experience is contained in a single group of six, seven, eight, or more? How many hundreds of hidden persons are brought to each group meeting, held in each participant's heart with loving concern? How many hidden prayers lie unspoken in a small group, waiting to come to the surface if only given an invitation? How many hundreds of times will the Holy Spirit flash forth in a word, facial expression, or movement of the heart? How many lifelong friendships does Christ want to form during the sacred time of meeting?

See what a responsibility the Small-Group Leader has! He or she needs to facilitate the occasion of grace that is the small-group meeting. To do this, such a leader needs to be a man or woman of prayer both before the meeting and especially during the meeting. Such a leader should pray for the members of the small group, asking the Lord to bless them. And such a leader should ask for the graces needed to recognize God's presence in fellow group members, hear the inspirations of the Holy Spirit, and preserve the bond of charity. He or she may also need some tips. And that's what we'll provide now.

1. Truly Listen. Yes, a Small-Group Leader will need to have questions ready and will have lots of things on his or her mind, but must fight the temptation to be distracted when someone is sharing his or her heart. The Holy Spirit rewards loving attention and will inspire a Small-Group Leader with the right questions when listening with his or her heart.

2. Acknowledge the Good. A Small-Group Leader might not be able to give a word of affirmation in response to everything that is said, but it is important for him or her to acknowledge what is shared — and it should be genuine. It may be helpful to say things like, "Thank you, Sally, for sharing that personal experience," or perhaps repeat back to the group what the person said: "Bob, that was really interesting there. You said..."

3. **Don't Push the Silent Participant.** Sometimes you'll have a participant who rarely speaks, or speaks only when asked. This could be out of shyness or habit, he or she could simply be listening and reflecting on what others are saying. Some people need several weeks to get comfortable enough to say anything. If they are put on the spot, even gently, they may be uncomfortable enough not to return. It's important to show warmth to the silent participant who may feel self-conscious of the fact that he or she is not opening up. Usually, when he or she feels safe and accepted, he or she will begin to open up on his or her own. So, while it's true that everyone should come to the meetings with a readiness to share, nobody should be pushed to do so.

Here's one simple way to invite the silent participant to speak: "Julie, it looks like you had something to say..." To do this genuinely, you'll want to monitor eye contact. Also, because many times silent people are forming their sentences in their minds before they speak, you might want to set up some quiet time up front. For example, you could say, "Okay, let's take 30 seconds and just think about this one as it is an especially good question." Then monitor the silent person's eye contact. Finally, affirming him or her when he or she does speak up gives the silent participant the confidence to continue to contribute.

4. **Lovingly Direct the Talkative Participant.** While some participants may be quiet, others may be quite lively and talkative. The challenge for the Small-Group Leader is to keep the talkative participant involved and excited but also to make sure that he or she doesn't dominate the conversation. The key is to direct his or her conversation, and this will take practice and patience. Here are a few examples of how to direct the conversation: If he or she is talking for too long, gently break in and say, "You're covering a lot of interesting (exciting, important, etc.) territory, Thomas. Let's back up a second and see if anyone else has something to add. What do you think, Judy?" Or, "Let's stop there, Luke. That's an interesting experience. Has anyone had a similar experience?" The principle is to lovingly direct the conversation of the talkative participant and to draw other participants back into the conversation.

5. **Hand Off the "Problem Person" to the Appropriate People.** It's rare, but it does happen. Someone in the group may engage in inappropriate sharing or repeatedly "off the wall" opinions. It's important that the Small-Group Leader bring in the priest or another pastoral leader for one-on-one guidance in dealing with the "problem person." The Small-Group Leader should also bring this person to the attention of the Program Coordinator.

Of course, not every "problem person" will require this kind of action. In some cases, it's simply a matter of someone being overly knowledgeable and they just need to be roped in and made part of the solution, perhaps an assistant to the leader. For example, you might take someone aside and say, "Wow, Mark, you know a ton about St. Thérèse, and that's great. Let's do this: I really need some help getting some of the members in the group to interact. How about if you and I remain quiet for the first 60 seconds and then, if no one is speaking, I'll nod to you and you can jump in with a relevant comment, but remember to really encourage the others to speak."

6. Attend to the Sometimes-Absent Participant. It's ideal that every participant attend every meeting, but sometimes this is not possible. So what do you do if a person misses one or more meetings? If the participant misses the first meeting, make sure you introduce him or her at the second meeting. If a participant misses any other meeting, you may want to arrange for him or her (and any other absentee members from other small groups) to come early to the next group meeting, and then play the DVD talk that was missed. Of course, you'll have to make sure that you can use the gathering room earlier and that you can come early to the next meeting to set up the DVD talk.

   If the participant misses the first two meetings, or two consecutive meetings, he or she may want to consider starting the program again, with another group. This would need to be his or her decision.

   Make sure that you cover the procedures for absences in your first group meeting. It's worth emphasizing that the presence and participation of each member is important.

7. Review the Ten Commandments for Small-Group Success. The Small-Group Leader should be well-versed in those commandments, which now follow.

# TEN COMMANDMENTS FOR SMALL-GROUP SUCCESS

1. Be willing to share. Participants should come to the meetings with a joyful readiness to share. The small-group experience depends on sharing. You never know how much something you share may help another. Sometimes you may not want to share, and that's okay.

2. Let others share. Everyone needs to be given an opportunity to share. Give others the chance to talk. Do not fear silence. No one person should dominate the small group's time with lengthy sharing, even if unintentional. It is the Small-Group Leader's role to ask people to observe this rule should someone get carried away.

3. Do your homework. Homework for *Divine Mercy in the Second Greatest Story Ever Told* consists of reviewing and reflecting on any of the questions that you don't cover during your small-group discussion. By reviewing those questions, you ensure that you are up-to-speed with the content, which will help you to better participate in later group discussion.

4. Stay focused. The small-group sessions are to be focused on viewing the video teaching, reading the prompts, and discussing the questions, not on personal problems, theological opinions, gossip, or promotion of a cause — even a worthy one.

5. Don't give advice. It is not appropriate to give advice to someone during the small-group sessions. If a person seeks advice from you, speak to one another at the end of the meeting.

6. Don't lecture. This is not a time for long lectures. However, the Small-Group Leader may need to explain something related to the subject matter at hand. Of course, it's also alright to share information that could illumine a given topic, but try to keep it succinct.

7. Be respectful. Everyone's experience is valid. If you disagree with something, do so respectfully and charitably. Never ridicule or cut down another person. When someone else is speaking, we should be listening.

8. Keep confidentiality. A promise of confidentiality is asked and expected of each group member, giving one another freedom to share sensitive feelings or personal information relevant to the topic and questions, if desired. However, this is not the time for confession or counseling.

9. Follow the leader. It is important to give support and cooperation to the Small-Group Leader who is charged with the responsibility of seeing that these group guidelines are followed.

10. Enjoy yourself!

# NOTES

# NOTES

# NOTES

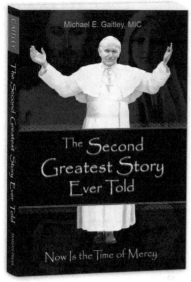

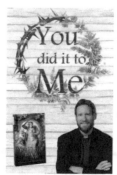

# Continue Your Small-group Journey with

# Fr. Michael Gaitley

**Hearts AFIRE**

Parish-based Programs from the
Marian Fathers of the Immaculate Conception

The Hearts Afire program is
changing my life.

— JAMES K.

Hearts Afire begins with a journey to the Immaculate Heart using the book *33 Days to Morning Glory* and its accompanying group-retreat program.

Mary then leads us to the Sacred Heart, which begins the second part of Stage One with the book *Consoling the Heart of Jesus* and its accompanying group-retreat program.

**Stage 1**

The Two Hearts
PART ONE:
The Immaculate Heart

PART TWO:
The Sacred Heart

Stage Two: Wisdom & Works of Mercy begins with *The 'One Thing' Is Three* and its accompanying group-study program, which gives group members a kind of crash course in Catholic theology. Stage Two concludes with a program for group works of mercy based on the bestselling book '*You Did It to Me.*'

**Stage 2**

Wisdom and Works of Mercy
PART ONE: Wisdom

PART TWO:
Works of Mercy

The heart of Stage Three: Keeping the Hearts Afire is the Marian Missionaries of Divine Mercy. Learn more about becoming a Marian Missionary. Here's How:

1. Get a FREE copy of the *Missionary Handbook* by Fr. Michael Gaitley.
   (Order today by calling 800–462–7426, code MMDBK, some restrictions apply.)

2. Visit MarianMissionaries.org or call 413-944-8500

**Stage 3**

**MARIAN MISSIONARIES**
*of*
**DIVINE MERCY**

AllHeartsAfire.org  •  1-877-200-4277